I0791491

Sublime Kudos

RICHARD FOLEY

BALBOA.PRESS

A DIVISION OF HAY HOUSE

Copyright © 2020 Richard Foley.

All rights reserved. No part of this book may be used or reproduced by any means, graphic, electronic, or mechanical, including photocopying, recording, taping or by any information storage retrieval system without the written permission of the author except in the case of brief quotations embodied in critical articles and reviews.

This book is a work of non-fiction. Unless otherwise noted, the author and the publisher make no explicit guarantees as to the accuracy of the information contained in this book and in some cases, names of people and places have been altered to protect their privacy.

Balboa Press books may be ordered through booksellers or by contacting:

Balboa Press
A Division of Hay House
1663 Liberty Drive
Bloomington, IN 47403
www.balboapress.com
844-682-1282

Because of the dynamic nature of the Internet, any web addresses or links contained in this book may have changed since publication and may no longer be valid. The views expressed in this work are solely those of the author and do not necessarily reflect the views of the publisher, and the publisher hereby disclaims any responsibility for them.

The author of this book does not dispense medical advice or prescribe the use of any technique as a form of treatment for physical, emotional, or medical problems without the advice of a physician, either directly or indirectly. The intent of the author is only to offer information of a general nature to help you in your quest for emotional and spiritual well-being. In the event you use any of the information in this book for yourself, which is your constitutional right, the author and the publisher assume no responsibility for your actions.

Any people depicted in stock imagery provided by Getty Images are models, and such images are being used for illustrative purposes only.
Certain stock imagery © Getty Images.

Print information available on the last page.

ISBN: 978-1-9822-5012-6 (sc)
ISBN: 978-1-9822-5013-3 (e)

Library of Congress Control Number: 2020911293

Balboa Press rev. date: 07/27/2020

Also by Richard Foley

Panchromatic Obscurity
Uncanny Miscellany

NOTE OF EXPLANATION:

Nonfiction is essential because it has such a significant impact. Fairy tales merely entertain us without etching bona fide lessons into our lives. Now I'm going to address a topic that would behoove us to heed…

FORMERLY THE DISTORTED SOUL,
RICHARD LAYTON FOLEY

Originally, this adaptable book was titled "Travesty of an Asylum." While I was writing this manuscript, I had an epiphany. Then the theme mutated from negative to positive. Bear with me as you read these pages. Watch the very thread of this publication unfold. Beyond legitimacy, mental institutions are a parody of a refuge. Although the mental health system is not perfect by any means whatsoever, it has improved immensely over time. Yet, it needs to grow even further! Screws were diligently driven into people's brains in an abortive attempt to get rid of their psychosis. Dunking people's heads into cold water until they either froze or drowned to death was done for the same purpose. Shackled and chained in an inevitable filthy environment, they urinated and defecated all over themselves with oblivion. Modernly, there are less peculiar methods and more effective therapy. Medication and counseling are *indeed* better than straitjackets and lobotomies, but mental patients are *still* mistreated remorselessly. Reporting the staff for these atrocities is futile and redundant because the mental patients are discredited due to being diagnosed with Bipolar Disorder, Schizophrenia, etc. If a staff member verbally or physically attacks a patient, that staff is "investigated" and exonerated simply because they claim the patient hallucinated the incident. Querying the validity of this is doubtful. Obviously, mental patients have experienced these symptoms. Subsequently, these mental patients are retaliated against via the staff who have lied to get them in trouble. Personal admissible items such as salt, pepper, sugar, and condiments are confiscated as contraband. Poised and ready, *some* staff are looking for any opportunity to harm the mental patients with a tendency to ruin their tranquility. Pompous signs that allege mental patients have plenty of rights are violated daily and have been posted all over walls of mental hospitals, offensively. Incorrigible staff have bribed despondent mental patients to do deeds of treachery against their own peers. Cigarettes, alcohol, drugs, food, and money are among the list of stuff that some of the mental patients have craved and will do *almost anything* to obtain. Fighting between the mental patients is instigated by some staff who are amused by this, and wager on the results. Drill sergeants could learn a thing or two from *some* of the staff who seem to be under the impression that mental hospitals are boot camps. Meticulously complaining about a wrinkle on somebody's bed, *some* staff will harass mental patients with petty nit-picking. Distraught from their predicaments, some mental patients should be handled with a more *appropriate* approach. Lousy staff frequently say their favorite rhetorical question: "Where do you think you are at, the Holiday Inn!" Honestly, who in the world would choose to be in a mental hospital voluntarily? Unless you are homeless, suicidal, or have deteriorated so vastly that you have no other alternative. Blatantly exploiting the mental patients with disdain so they vow to never return is *some* staff's primary philosophy. Gee whiz, the employees of mental institutions *literally* get paid to destroy the mental patients' vitality! Since staff are not considered expendable, they can do *basically* whatever they want, and get away scot-free. Zero consequences follow them; they don't even get reprimanded slightly! Shirking their benevolent duty by calling their colleagues to let them know they are not coming to work that day; the staff will not get fired; this is their "prerogative." Nowhere else is this condoned! Candidly, most of the staff merely have jobs in mental hospitals because they get health insurance. Please don't get me wrong, a few of the staff are *more than* decent. Succoring low functioning vulnerable mental patients whom I have advocated for with altruism has been a noble token of integrity. Albeit, I am nothing, but a sinner rescued by grace. Ephesians 2:8-9. Wondering why God hasn't wiped mental hospitals off the globe, I have inquired Him about injustice. Behold, evil mental hospitals have not deserved to remain intact and ought to be atomized! After, everybody has been evacuated, of course. Often, I ask God: "Why does mental illness even exist?" Always, I have received the same answer. Saturated in turpitude like a sponge in water, we deviated from God's natural path of harmony. Genetically bequeathing us with an immoral inheritance, Adam and Eve have cursed and plagued humanity. Plus, Jesus Christ revolutionized what Adam and Eve did in the Garden of Eden for our sake. Romans 5:12-21. Compared to Jesus Christ, we all have struggled with pride and are in a starkly stagnant category. Habitually measured by a common misconception, you might think you are immune to mental illness, think again. You're not! Nobody is! Mental illness has not discriminated. Mental illness doesn't care how smart or intelligent you are. Mental illness doesn't care how strong or brawny you are. Mental illness doesn't care how handsome or pretty you are. Mental illness doesn't care how successful or prosperous you are. Mental illness *just* doesn't care! Many theories are floating around out there, but nobody *really* knows for *certain* how people become mentally ill. Heredity or alcohol and drug induced or traumatized from tragedies. Perhaps some of these combined together are accurate, but there is inadequate evidence for it to be substantiated. Maybe none of them are. Either way, some people who are mentally ill didn't have any of those things occur to them. Despite how people develop a mental illness, most people don't know much about it. Nor do they care to. Unfortunately, the mentally ill are considered the dregs of society, inferior creatures, pathetic vermin, etc. Erroneously, the mentally ill are stereotyped and stigmatized. Notoriously derogatory labels such as crazy, dumb, stupid, and retarded, have spread abroad. Generally, people are not concerned about a subject that appears to be irrelevant, until it affects them directly. Dangerous prescriptions are forced down patients' throats with a litany of serious side effects. Experimenting on these mental patients like guinea pigs with machinations is a scandalously lucrative occupation. Poverty-stricken, *some* mental patients do not have the luxury of eating scrumptious food at the canteen, and they therefore go haywire and have splurged their indigent funds. Whether inmates are adjudicated "Not Guilty by Reasons of Insanity" or are found "Incompetent to Proceed Trial" for their crimes, they are sentenced to a mental hospital indefinitely for punishment. Quite frankly, the criteria for forensic patients to get discharged is hogwash! Citizens who are on mental health probation and speak or do something that is not illegal but unorthodox, are whisked away with usurpations. Steady duress has pressured these forensic patients with a flippancy that has orchestrated their Achilles' heel. Regardless of what sort of mental patient they are, forensic or civil, violent patients and calm patients should be separated because that is only fair. Haplessly blending them together is a contradictory mixture! Yet, they do it anyway! Alienated from normalcy, mental patients have tolerated each other's personalities with difficulty. Fetid stinky odor lingers through the halls because *some* patients have poor hygiene. Lack of showering, brushing their teeth, and flushing the toilets are *just* a few of the unsanitary conditions that must be endured. Combating the controversy, mental patients are divided rather than united because their enemy has wedged fear between them with wrath. Sadistically tortured by morbid patterns, mental patients have welcomed euthanasia! Chronically wishing that these unsavory Machiavellian mental institutions are pulverized into a powdery substance, I haven't minced words! Okay, so this doesn't get misconstrued, I have not insinuated that I have a desire for carnage, I *just* want the establishments themselves, and what they represent annihilated. Dignity is not structured inside mental institutions, and it probably never will be due to phlegm. Roaming through these trivial labyrinths, these mental patients have chased some expectations away by smearing them with disappointments. Amazed by a maze, we gauged mental hospitals are cesspools. Shoved over the edge by a harrowing memory that guides these mental patients into agony, they barely maintain their composure. Security guards beat patients to a bloody pulp and brag about it with enthusiasm! Cameras are installed to record altercations, but *who* has access to the footage? Alas, patients are in hospitals to get better, not worse! Doctors heal the sick, not the well. Silhouetted in fortitude, Jesus Christ is the panacea that cures with sanctification! Luke 5:30-32. Psychiatrists and psychologists bask in narcissism because they have graduated from college with a silly notion that they are cardinal. Insisting that sage individuals have figured God out is bogus because uneducated individuals comprehend God through Jesus' atonement. Matthew 11:25-27. 1 Corinthians 1:26-31. 1 John 2:1-6. Quacks, charlatans, and frauds have schemed patients without a license! Shrugging with nonchalance, nurses deny patients medical supplies, unless it is an emergency, so they won't get sued. Propaganda is cheerfully celebrated and it lurks around every corner. Dissecting a conspiracy that has settled for paranoia is befitting! Silenced by poignancy, mental patients have no strategy! Ennui has paralyzed mental patients with apprehension! Engrossed in fancy materialism has manipulated us amid an illusion of secularism. Debunking Christianity is trendy, but pointless. Study the Bible and monitor the prophecy that is fulfilled. Bridged from darkness to light, Jesus Christ is the cusp between heathens and saints. Psalms 18:28. Isaiah 9:2. John 1:5. John 8:12. John 12:46. 2 Corinthians 4:6. 1 Peter 2:9. 1 John 1:5-10. Sand is flowing down in the hourglass as the pendulum of entropy swings back and forth between incarceration and liberty. Mulling over the gulf between staff and patients, I have not paused to be the harbinger of virtues! Ransoming these hostages from their captivity would be a pity for the mental health system's persnickety hocus-pocus because it would be exposed! Weighing the pros and cons of mental institutions with cogitation is vain because optimism is light, and pessimism is heavy. Insensitive to patients, the staff's attitudes will never be changed at this rate! Painting such intense vivid pictures of a misfeasance, there is no cliff-hanger included at the end, and the only mystery is why this paradox has continued? Meshing faulty protocols with sturdy procedures is *just* a reverie! Persecuted by the staff, mental patients have hesitated to grant other patients grub because *technically* it is disobeying the rules! Ambivalence has crippled me indecisive. Proverbs 22:9. Romans 13:1-5. Ostensibly, mental hospitals have accommodated patients with recovery, and at that, I have glanced askance! Strutting around with their metaphorical astigmatism, the staff have believed they will be exempt from being judged by the Almighty. Atheists and agnostics are only those who have not experienced the Lord's glory hitherto! Presto, God's legacy, His Son, Jesus Christ, is the epitome of a role model! John 13:15. 1 Peter 2:21. Curiosity has arrived and interfered with the League of Degeneracy, but who has the upper hand? Suddenly mustering resiliency, mental patients should have reversed this momentum into an instrument of robust activity! Eureka, I am not the only one who has fantasized about mental hospitals getting bulldozed! Lavish mental patients have persistently hoped that they get avenged! Pregnant mental patients have miscarriages due to neglect from the staff who try to keep this hush-hush. Rendering mental hospitals obsolete, God will diminish them into rubble! Rubbernecking at the debris of mental institutions would be splendid! After the administration and honchos of mental hospitals have waved the white flag with a condign equilibrium, and their shadows have gestured surrender, I will delight in enrichment! Roll out the red carpet for relinquishment! Sighing with relief is *just* a distant dream! Pandemonium has dominated serenity! Pipe down or snap? Irrefutably, it is the latter. Pious Pharisees incessantly accused Jesus Christ of heresy and blasphemy. Herod Antipas derided Jesus Christ, and Pontius Pilate had pined for Him to be released, but the mob was vociferous and were shouting otherwise. Whipping Jesus could not thwart His ministry! Lacerated and bruised, He was and *is* dauntless! Murdering the Messiah, Jesus Christ to get rid of Him was to no avail due to His resurrection! Empowering us with a clean slate, God fills the vacuum of our psyche! Ticking from one number to another, the clock has chimed in with a chip on its shoulder.

Patronized by mental health professionals, mental patients have been defined as loose cannons. Caged up like feral animals, mental patients cannot be tamed because they are Homo sapiens, not elements of a zoo! Reaching through the barbed wire fences of jails and prisons and mental institutions, Jesus Christ brings genuine freedom! John 14:6. John 8:32. Scolding mental patients for hugging and kissing consensually like affection is leprosy, *some* of the staff are ridiculous! Balanced by this last resort, patients have masturbated because they are deprived of sex with the other gender. Stooping to another level of companionship because they get lonely *just* like everybody else, mental patients have sabotaged their relationships with flagrant selfishness. Convinced they have spared their mates from pain; mental patients have obliterated their partner's hearts and any chance of contentment. Encountering my lovelorn emotions with shards of intimacy, my relationships *have been* disastrous fiascoes! Nostalgia has collided with skepticism and cynicism. Mawkish sentiment is like beachcombers collecting shrapnel ashore, it's otiose. Crying with hysteria because my heart was punctured by ruses that were camouflaged as love, I was yearning for amnesia. Hanging me from the gallows would be paradise in contrast to marrying my ex-fiancées! Exquisitely charming noose *would have been* just dandy! Lynching me *would've* been a rubber stamp for a pardon! Instead, the Lord my God has jubilantly resuscitated and revived me like a volcanic eruption! Psalm 34:18. Psalm 147:3. Beseeching the Lord for a miracle, I had been spiraling through a slipshod vortex of melancholy. Pinching clay from His celestial pottery, God shapes us into His masterpiece. Isaiah 64:8. Jeremiah 18:6. Deciphering this ambiguous exegesis might be grueling, but I reckon it's the whole shebang. Faced with such an ugly monstrous reflection in the mirror, I glared through a superstitious kamikaze phantom… Haughty uppity critics who have a nasty knack for slandering the Lord's reputation because they are not objective, should check out, "Jesus: The Great Debate" by Dr. Grant R. Jeffery. Digesting this archaeological scholarly phenomenal testimony will be a recipe for a cosmopolitan assessment. Tangible reliable doctrines have proselytized infidels into worshippers of Jehovah! Inexorably refusing to accept that Jesus of Nazareth is who His disciples announced He was and *is*, makes less sense than listening to a garbled commentary. Medieval artists could not have forged the image that is on the Shroud of Turin. Iron oxide was unavailable until two centuries ago. Hence, it cannot be the ingredient some claim was detected on the surface of the linen cloth. Fables, legends, and myths have exaggerated their characters with fallacy. Golgotha and the empty tomb of Jesus Christ is assumed and speculated to be at the site of the ancient church of the Holy Sepulcher, but most likely they are geographically located in Jerusalem. Ouch, the staff has no conscience because they are antinomians! Vouching for the ornery officious mental health system is like an idiot jumping out of an airplane without a parachute! Places that are supposed to help folks have done *just* the opposite. Barricaded by the herculean obstacles of tyranny has been bothering these mental patients to an abominable degree. Landing atop a mountain in a hot air balloon is cheating because we intentionally skip the necessary clogs and hard work it takes to become triumphant. Instead, we must start at the bottom and climb up to the peak of ultimate victory. When we reach the summit, we will find an award that was earned for us by somebody else. Zealously, we ought to run as fast as we can! Although somebody greater than us has already won the prize! Jesus Christ has achieved the most remarkable championship! Rushing toward the finish line to grab the gold medal, we have stumbled upon a monumental discovery. Paraphrased into a more accurate statement, it is not *just* a serendipitous coincidence! Behold, it is divine intervention! Standing there at the finish line with the gold medal, Jesus Christ is eagerly waiting to meet us at such a suitable rendezvous! Since we are incapable of meriting our forgiveness and salvation because it is a gift, we can merely be grateful for God's mercy. Anchoring such legalism has not dispensed grace, in a nutshell. Soldiers who have battled against each other in war generally obtain scars. Evangelism is not blossoming within mental hospitals because there is a famine of chaplaincy. Confined to jails, prisons, and mental hospitals, inmates and patients are on the brink of apostasy. Converting pagans to monotheism hinges on how ironclad our connection with God is, or the deficiency thereof. Inserting the skeleton key, which is God, into every door to unlock the mecca of subsistence, is pivotal! Clutch God for a prompt symmetry! Weeping from our mother's womb with an intuition that life is going to be flinty, we knew that we would not have the proper equipment. Automatically, we somehow knew what we were getting ourselves into from infancy. Squirming away from our tribulations, we have all gone astray, and Jesus Christ is our scapegoat. Isaiah 53:6. Alright, these extravagant words must be pruned. I'm going to branch out by penning freely. Mental hospitals are not about the mental patients getting rehabilitated; they are about liability. For instance: When a mental patient chokes on a specific sort of food, it is not served anymore. If a patient chokes on peanut butter, patients will never get peanut butter again. If a patient chokes on a hot dog, patients will never get hot dogs again. If somebody chokes on pizza, I'm going to be pissed off! So, on and so forth. Preposterous! Anybody could choke on anything! Any kind of food! If we choke on everything, are they going to get rid of everything?! What would we eat?! Each other?! Hooray for cannibalism! What would they do, get rid of us, the patients?! If they could get away with feeding us through our veins, they would! They feed us *something* so they can put a check in a box, *just* like everything *else* in mental hospitals, or should I say, *just* like everything *else* in the mental health system. If we strangled ourselves or another patient via a belt, all belts would be banned. If a patient pierced themselves or another patient with an ink pen, you could say farewell to ink pens. Therefore, mental patients use crayons! Can you fathom writing a lawyer or another professional business a letter in crayon?! After the lawyer or whoever receives the letter in the mail, acknowledges that the return address belongs to a mental hospital, and that it is written in crayon, it will probably be disposed of! Taxpayers would be livid if they knew how their dollars were being wasted! Every patient will be disciplined for one patient who misbehaved. *Some* mental patients end up committing suicide because *some* staff members treat them so harshly! *Some* mental patients get out of mental hospitals and need help but are scared to say anything to anyone because they might get put back in a mental hospital again! *Most people* assume that all mental patients are completely out of their minds. Such is not the case. *Some* mental patients can't get out of mental hospitals due to their judges are so stuck on the patient's past. There is no leeway for misunderstandings. When a judge simply sees something that looks good on paper but not actually what took place, they really don't get the gist of it. Staff members wallop patients who merely defend themselves, but *who* has the pen? Indeed, the pen is mightier than the sword! Staff document this as revenge instead of what it really is, self-defense. *Who* do you think the *judge* is going to listen to, the *staff*, or the *patients*? I mean sure there are *all sorts* of people mental patients contact to get something done about all this, but *none* of them will *really* help. Governmental officials, human rights organizations, lawyers, police, etc. People drive by mental hospitals in their vehicles, see the sign that says hospital, and they grin. "Oh, it's a hospital, they help people." Yet, they cannot *possibly imagine* what is really going on in there! *Every single day… Invisible scars are the worst…* People look at you every day, but they don't see, they don't know, and they don't care! This doesn't pertain to *just* mental patients. There are people we see every day that we look at. We look right through them, right past their pain, we have gazed to what's behind them, like they aren't even there…. You might even be one of these people that other people don't seem to see. I guess we don't see *them* because we got our *own* problems…. Sorry if I have rambled from one tangent to another with an esoteric jargon. Once upon a time, there was a dude who ended too many sentences with exclamation points! He guaranteed everybody he would never end another sentence with an exclamation point again! Especially a bunch of 'em!!!!!!!!!!!!!!!!!!!!!! Strumming a fiddle, we won't crack this riddle, if we just sit around and piddle. Mental patients run out of mental patience. I'm not a laureate, but I do know that God is in every nook and cranny because He is omnipresent. Sailing across uncharted territory with a crystalline shipwreck is ludicrous, but we do it anyway notwithstanding good counsel! I had to lose my mind to gain my purpose! Racism is such a rancorous pestilence. Myriad people have not acknowledged that *every* race is persecuted. Would you hold a grudge against an immigrant who did something bad to another immigrant? No! So, why do we hold a grudge against another race because their ancestors did something bad to ours? What's the difference? Nothing! Both were strangers. We did not know either. Even if we did, it still doesn't matter, it was a long time ago. Tit for tat? Heads or tails? Flip a coin? Skateboarding through a minefield, or brainwashing toddlers? I have observed numerous folks quarreling over what color skin Jesus Christ had. African Americans swear He was black. Caucasians swear He was white. I hate to burst everybody's bubble, but Jesus was a Jew, so He was olive. What difference does it make?! I don't care if Jesus Christ was purple! His blood was red like ours, and He shed it for everybody! Jews and gentiles alike! Thus far all this might seem like just a screed, an incredulous hyperbole, but it's not to be taken figuratively; I can be quoted verbatim. Athleticism was instilled and ingrained into me by my brother. Thanks Jeff, you created a monster! Thank God you did, though! Otherwise, I would not have survived. God divulged a secret to me; life is like sports. We must be relentlessly determined to win! Jeffery Foley, my brother, trained me to never give up! Programmed like adamant machines to never quit, we will reap what we sow. 2 Corinthians 9:6. Burning the towel so we cannot throw it in, would be savvy! Although I participated in countless sports, I was only good at a diminutive amount of them, and only two of them were I a medalist. Baseball, basketball, soccer, golf, bowling, and billiards have never been my forte. Wrestling, football, and swimming were my mastery. Volleyball and ping-pong have become my expertise. Addicted to winning medals in wrestling and swimming had been my lofty premiums. Jeffery Foley, my brother, imprinted valor into me. When I wrestled, if I was losing by a bunch of points, and there was only one second left, I knew I didn't have enough time to score ample points to come back and win, but I certainly strived to somehow flip my opponent on his back to pin him. Sometimes I did. Sometimes I did not. Or if I was losing by a lot of points and I had enough time to beat my opponent via points, and he was too formidable to pin, I would endeavor to score a point by an escape, or I would try to score two points by a reversal or a takedown, or I would attempt to score three points by a near fall. Sometimes

I did. Sometimes I did not. When I swam, it did not matter how many swimmers were ahead of me, which I don't mean to be boastful, but were usually none; I swam like I had a starved shark or crocodile behind me with a ravenous titanic appetite. If another swimmer or swimmers were within an inch of touching victory, I would still attempt to harness enough speed to exceed him or them. Sometimes I did. Sometimes I did not. When I played football, I never dodged the big guys, I invariably went towards them. When I was on offense, even though I was small, I ran into the big guys with moxie. When I was on defense, even though I was small, I tackled the big guys like I was a juggernaut. Irrefutably, I was never the largest fellow, but I had the heart of a lion! It did not matter how many points I was losing by, I pledged to make a comeback. Sometimes I did. Sometimes I did not. When I play volleyball and ping-pong, it doesn't matter how far out of range the ball goes, I'll kill myself, and even more than that just to hit the ball back over the net. Sometimes I do. Sometimes I don't. Squinting to see the volleyball because the sun is too bright, hit the shadow because the shadow is the volleyball. Despite me winning matches, meets, and games, I still felt like a loser! I was! Innately, we all are. When we accept Jesus Christ as our Lord and Savior, we become winners in less than a jiffy! Who are you? Are you a loser? Are you a winner? Hebrews 12:1-4 Matthew 5:12. 1 Corinthians 15:50-58. Do you believe in the Lord Jesus Christ? He believes in you! I have a friend who is relentlessly determined when we play sports together and as we hike through life with God together. Literally, we would play volleyball for hours! We would hit the ball back and forth until we lost track of time. Until time was irrelevant. Victory was the only thing that mattered. This friend of mine, got everybody involved; he encouraged people by giving them snacks for playing sports. Which I really liked because I cherish oatmeal pies! My friend included *even* the people who were *considered* misfits! Sound familiar? Jesus did that! Jesus does that still! *Step one…* Jesus Christ was, and *still* is relentlessly determined to win us, to win our hearts! Sit still for a moment, let this sink in. Jesus is always the solution to every problem. Although Jesus Christ is always the answer, He might teach us to do something different, but in the same way. Sometimes I have improvised. Rumor has it that I was *officially* allergic to sobriety. Hooked on tobacco, alcohol, and drugs, I bounced in and out jails, rehabs, and mental hospitals with recidivism, and I had bats in the belfry. Leisurely, I binged on these stimulants and narcotics and hallucinogens, the draconic agents of a cerebral catastrophe. Frying my brain on a gallimaufry of alcohol and drugs and stabbing a guy with a knife were not in the blueprints of my agenda, but I did them anyway, it was an ignominy. Apologetically, I confess this isn't an unvarnished motif because it has gone from how fouled up mental hospitals are to how wonderful God is, but that's mandatory, it has described the stages of this enlightened transformation. Vindicated by the Lamb of God, Christians should be hyped up with alacrity! Enthroned everywhere, God is riveting on us through His lens of transparency. Christians are tools of God; hammers, wrenches, screwdrivers, vises, tape measures, etc. Scriptures memorized without applying them is vanity. You can't win the lottery if you do not buy a ticket. Who is your favorite superhero? How much has he or she sacrificed? Would he or she die for you? Would they die for the world? If they did, would it be enough? Are they righteous enough? Are they impeccable? They must be for us to be salvaged! Since God is so supreme, He cannot permit any sin into Heaven, to God, it is infra dig. Splitting us apart from God, our sins have been putrid. Although our favorite superheroes are gallant, they are still chimerical and blemished. Jesus Christ is my favorite superhero because He is sterling! What if our favorite superheroes let us down? What if Wolverine was electrocuted because he inserted his claws into a wall socket because his metal alloy was regulated by Magneto? What if Red Skull chomped Captain America's shield into fragments, and spit them out with a defiant snarl? What if Red Skull guillotined Captain America? What if Bane unmasked Batman, revealing Bruce Wayne? What if Batman, Bruce Wayne, was more bat than man? What if

Bane scythed Batman to death? What if Lex Luthor weaponized Kryptonite? What if Lex Luthor somehow cajoled General Zod to step aside as Lex decapitated Superman with a sword of Kryptonite? What if our favorite superheroes flourish? Will it be enough? What if Wolverine invented a time machine and went back into the past to alter the future? What if Wolverine mechanically entrenched a latent bomb within Magneto that was activated when Magneto obnoxiously aggravated Wolverine by controlling his metal alloy? What if that bomb detonated, and Magneto exploded into smithereens? What if Red Skull gobbled Captain America's shield along with the osmotic venom that was furtively implanted into the shield? What if Captain America mortally poisoned Red Skull? What if Batman hewed Bane's mask off with an ax? What if Bane suffocated because he was unable to fix his mask? What if rabidly shooing Lex Luthor away was a cinch for Superman because he used the lasers from his eyes? What if Superman grappled with General Zod, and they fell into a vat of liquid Kryptonite? What if it was like boiling acid, melting them into some extraterrestrial gooey plasma? What if Jesus Christ is the only superhero that matters? What if you are fatigued from me starting these sentences with what if? What if from here on out, I begin and end every sentence with what if? Attentively espy the movie: "Batman v Superman: Dawn of Justice" and be acquainted with a similar irony. Heroes battled against each other like villains with a vendetta that was fueling vigilantism. Lex Luthor played Batman and Superman as pawns. Identifying with Jesus Christ, Superman sacrificed himself as he utilized a spear that had the potential to kill the Man of Steel. Valiantly, Superman terminated a fiendish beast named Doomsday and himself in the painstaking process. Robed in majesty, Jesus Christ is the "Superman" who sacrificed Himself on that rugged cross! Hebrews 1:1-4. 10:10-14. Colossians 2:14. Deliverance from our "Doomsday" is provided for through our repentance and faith! Acts 20:20-21. Chapters have no raison d'être. Unilateral bureaucracy has only simulated etiquette. What am I talking about? What is my cryptic message? Rise poetic psychosomatic ecstasy! *Meds for the heads! No cope without dope! Swallow your pills as you follow your thrills! Costly hugs, free drugs!* Debacles are prevalent; children are sodomized and molested by pedophiles. Abductors kidnap people. Folks get raped. Vehicles wreck. Folks get amputated. Suicides, homicides, and genocides. Folks get mutilated. Hurricanes, earthquakes, and tornados. Blizzards, wildfires, and tsunamis. Folks are bereaved. Jesus Christ is the prerequisite to carte blanche. Sin=calamity. Jesus Christ=vicarious propitiation. True strength is not demonstrated by being macho and hostile, that is just a misplaced virile façade. True strength is evinced by being mature enough to do what is right, notwithstanding marathon fads of iniquity. Physical strength is not for us to harm other people or do whatever we want with it. Physical strength is given to us by God to help other people, work jobs, play sports, and *stack up towers of blueberry pancakes!* If we have woe, we might not feel like grinning on the outside, but that doesn't mean we don't have an inner joy. We do not have to see joy for it to be there, we can't see God, yet we know He is there.... Christians who work in the mental health field or anywhere that is knavish, really need to stand up with action! "Hello, Mrs. Diabetes. Hey, Mrs. Schizophrenia. Hello, Mr. Cancer. Hey, Mr. Bipolar." Mental illness is something people have; it has not *defined* who we are, though! Jesus Christ has assembled Christians de novo! Clinically riotous, the mental health system has crevices and fissures that have arranged clichéd credence! Everything we are good at is because God has given us the ability to do so! If you died today, where would you go? Heaven or Hell? Do you know you can know? 1 John 5:13. You don't have to worry about it. You don't have to think about it. You can know it! Trying to earn your way to Heaven is an insult to the Lord Jesus Christ! God has imputed Christians. Romans 4:4-8. Toiling to get to Heaven is a gaffe. Romans 3:20-26. If you are going to keep some of the law, you must keep it all. Galatians 3:10-14. James 2:10-13. Jesus Christ not only nailed our sins to the cross, but the law we could not keep withal. Colossians

2:13-15. God knew we could never keep the law; that is why He sent His Son, Jesus Christ, to do it for us. Galatians 3:15-26. Jesus Christ completed the law. John 19:30. If we could keep the law, Jesus died for nothing. Galatians 2:21. Jesus Christ seals us. 1 Peter 1:3-5. Soap and water are our works and if we bathed in them, they would not wash our sins away, only the blood of Jesus Christ can do such a thing. Revelation 1:5. Everybody sins so nobody can get to Heaven by works. Ecclesiastes 7:20. How can we live in peace if we have tiptoed on eggshells, nervous that our sins have eclipsed our deeds? Romans 5:1-2. How in the heck can we be saved by faith *and* works? How can men have shaven beards? How can women have short long plaits? How can something be thin thick? How can the temperature be cold hot? Warranting that we indubitably are saved by faith *and* works is a crafty perverse oxymoron! Romans 11:6. If we are saved by faith *and* works, Jesus will be the only one in Heaven! If you have not accepted Jesus Christ as your Lord and Savior personally, and want to, pray something like this: "God I know I'm a sinner, I believe I'm incapable of living a sinless life, which is the only way anybody could join you in Heaven. I believe there is only one person who has ever lived a sinless life, Your Son, Jesus Christ. I believe He died on the cross for my personal sins, was buried, and rose from the grave." Congratulations! Scrub the glossy superficial decorum off mental hospitals by harnessing the Holy Spirit, and I will be giddy! Coarsely, the toilet paper mental patients have is like sandpaper! Seasonally, mental hospitals host carnivals. All the mental patients who have participated in this shindig get souvenirs to mark the festival. Likewise, this is the paragon of Jesus Christ! Tallying up our sins is not God's career. God is notching love in us through Jesus! Jesus Christ tips the scales of our destiny! "You should write a book about your life!" Everybody has importuned me. You have only glimpsed into my life in this book.... If I were to write my autobiography, you would hanker to be disintegrated! I won't do it! Lest there be a visceral upheaval! Warping my soul awry, my cuckoo life has been gruesome. Furnishing a quandary might seem like my priority, but I have equivocated holistically, and I am only flirting with clarity, that's not a lady. Accosting the mental health system's moot rote is like putting a square peg into a round hole! Loopholes could not get Andrew Laeddis back on the ferry to Boston, in "Shutter Island." Bottled up inside me was a fallow love for Lucinda that has been honed into a fertile dimension! Magnetically, Lucinda captured my heart with fetching love! Wooing Lucinda with God's unfailing love has been an enterprise for me, but I implored God for chutzpah! Hypnotized by Lucinda, my mangled fragile fidgety heart has vibrated like a torrential jackhammer that has surged through me with a nuptial rhapsody! Although I have certainly loved many women in my life, only one takes the cake. There's just something about Lucinda. She is… Gadzooks, the jig is up! Forfeiting His own life for us, Jesus Christ was elevated to the utmost grandeur! Avaricious proprietors of group homes and assisted living have embezzled the mentally ill's social security income with despotism! Flaying the artificiality off these phony extortionists would be superb, they have shaken the hands of their casualties and smiled right in front of them with plastic radicalism! Discombobulated by the mental health system's hypocrisy, I have doodled about a ton of their victims! Exalting God unremittingly, we have breathed oxygen through the valve of life with a rhythmic rapport! Taboo lopsided loony bins have finessed people with their chicanery! Squelching the rigmarole of parleying with padded cells would keep a dismal migraine at bay. Matching the mental health field to anything would be unfeasible because it is unparalleled to the whole kit and caboodle. Counterfeit ersatz versions of the real McCoy should be eliminated! Blankly, I have gaped at mental hospitals with a bewilderment that has regaled miffed pragmatism! Malpractice cannot be notarized! Entrepreneurs, nabobs, and tycoons of mental health vocations have haggled over pelf; they should stutter in retreat! Clashing against *their* sleazy unconstitutional mental health system has been like running on an amaranthine errand… Friction between mental hospitals and mental patients has been bonkers! Splintery aftermath of the mental health system should be afoot, but God has been delaying... Polishing mental hospitals up should be traded for the dialect of gobbledygook. Tampering with *their* saccharine pet mental health system is drivel! Callously tagged by the blistering verdict, "Not Guilty by Reasons of Insanity," with an encompassing jurisdiction, I have been trapped in the web of the mental health system for eons.... Hollywood has theatrically and falsely portrayed mental hospitals as palaces! Yikes, the hives of plutocracy in mental health have snaked through melees like a main circuit cable, plugging me straight into a spigot of napalm! Hats off to the boorish mental health system, it is up to par. Yahoos of mental health have tuned out litigation. Wow, mental hospitals are farces of havens that have polluted and contaminated their patients with a lethal infamy! Initially, this manuscript was to pinpoint the dearth of philanthropy in mental hospitals, but somewhere along the route, it digressed into something *much* more important. Previously mentioning the demolition of mental hospitals has been emphasized too much because it does not manifest what is chief. However, in retrospect I can view this from another angle. Eloquently venting my venomous resentments by rashly jotting them down on paper will not accomplish anything beneficial. Boomeranging back at me like bullets that ricochet, my complaints are bankrupt. Shifting the very fabric of this publication should have accentuated the gravity of adjustments. Yesterday has faded. Today is here. Tomorrow is nigh. Leading up to these crucial crossroads, we should be motivated by an initiative to give others an incentive to layer on ethical standards. Challenged by the ghastly status quo, we need to conquer it, not vice versa! During the mayhem, we must tenaciously cling to the Lord for integral nourishment. Selectively influenced by God, we should not permit the Devil to hijack us with an irresistible temptation. Consulting with God about everything is only logical… Focusing on God is the sine qua non! According to our pure reality, Jesus Christ is the remedy that has reverberated throughout history with laudable prestige!

Gallery of

Abstract Symbols

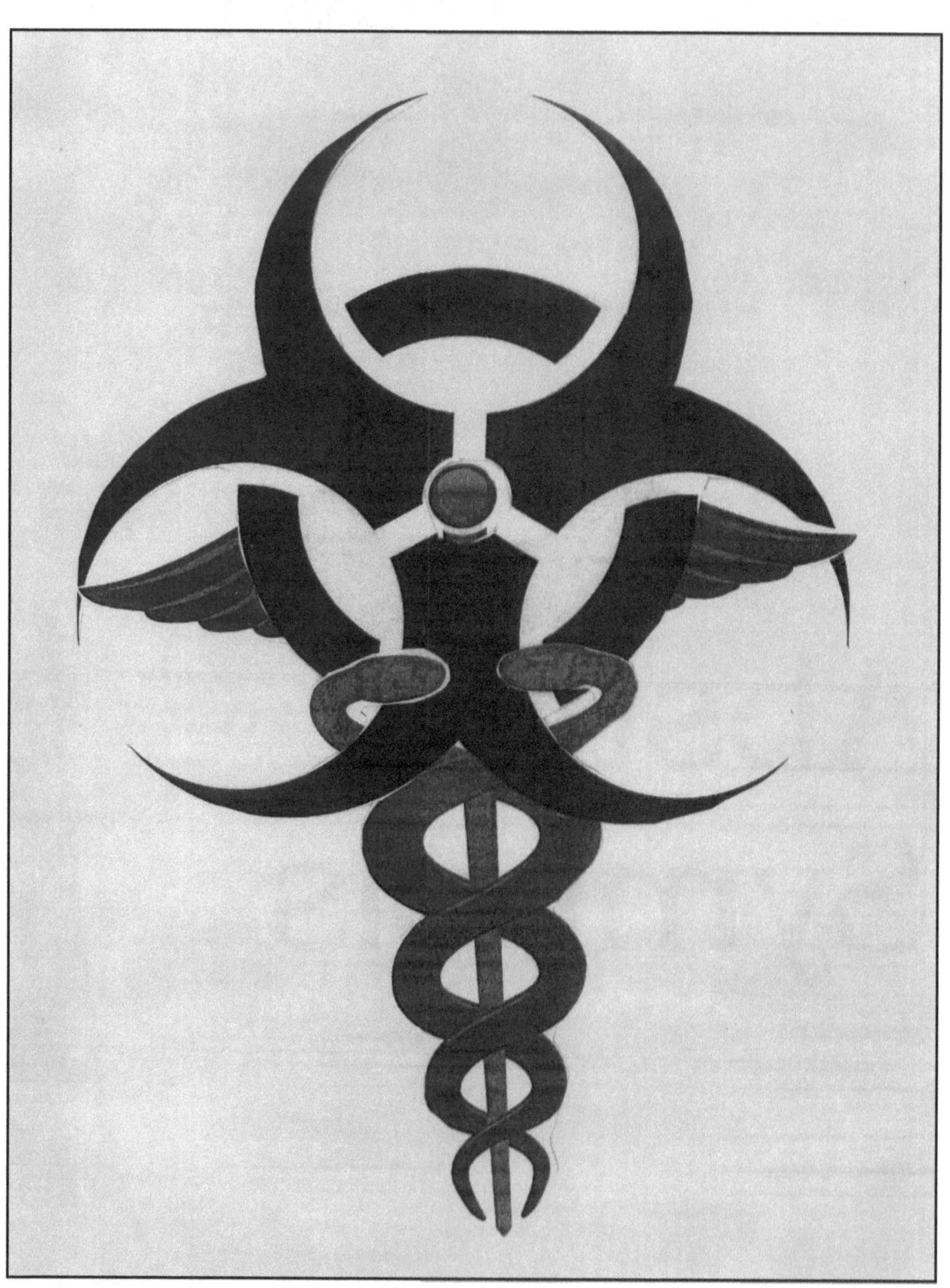

By: Tina Waltman

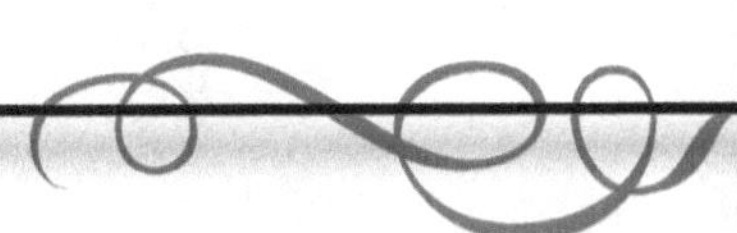

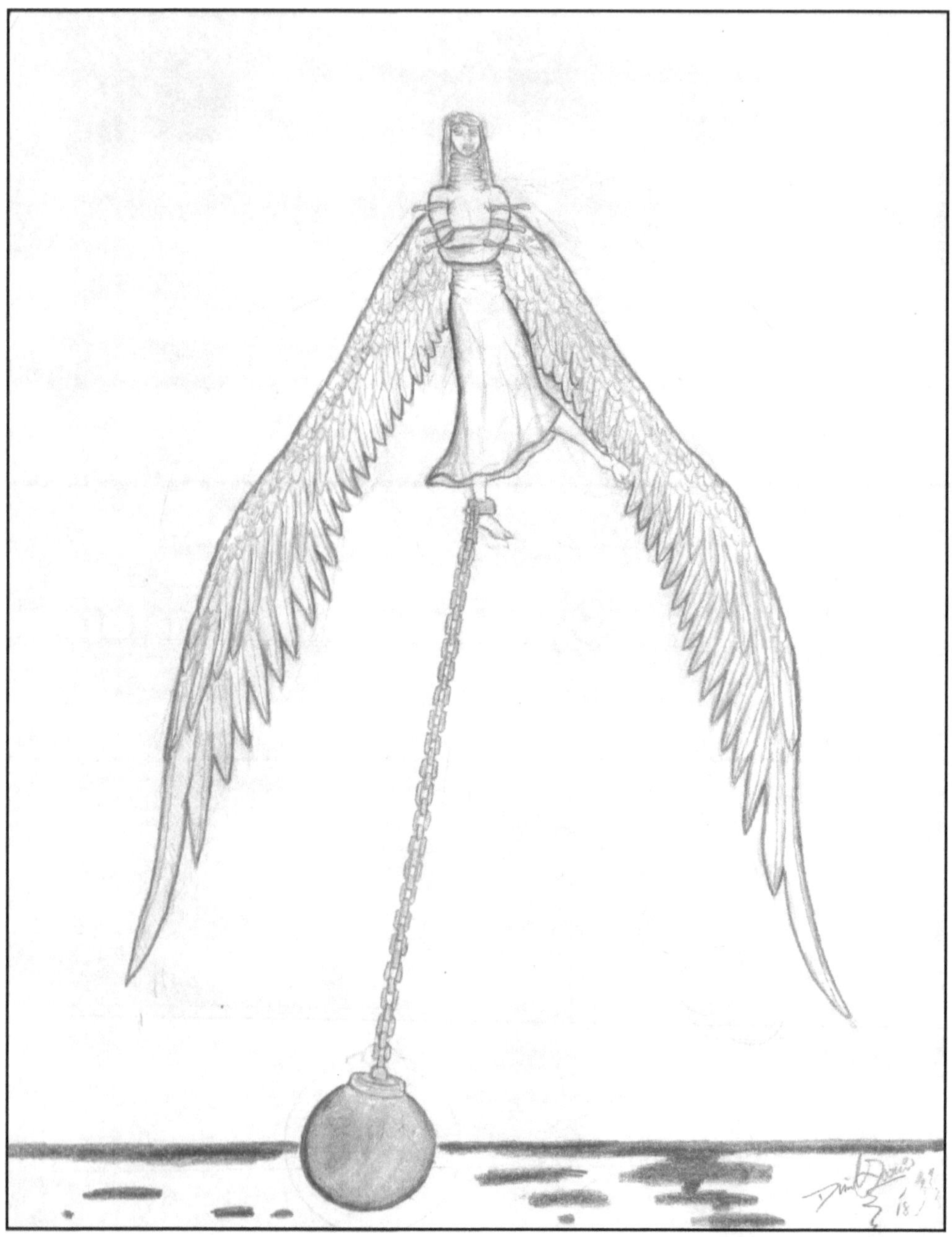

By: David Gracia

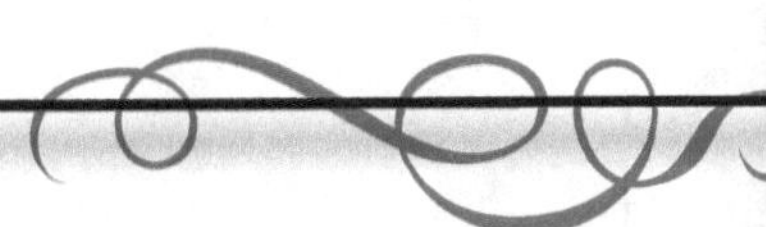

By: Thomas Crane

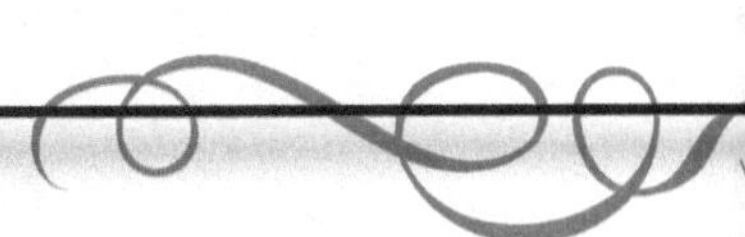

By: Demetrious Leonard Edwards Jr.

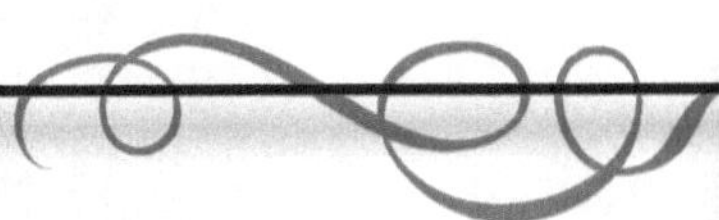

By: Michael D. Watkins

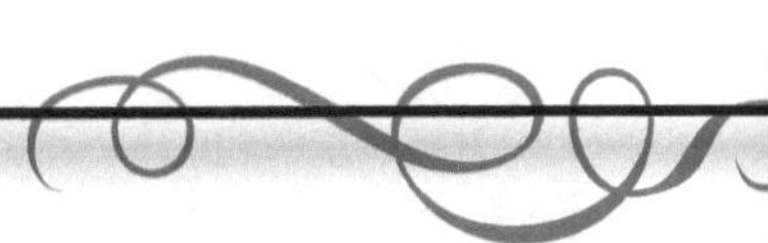

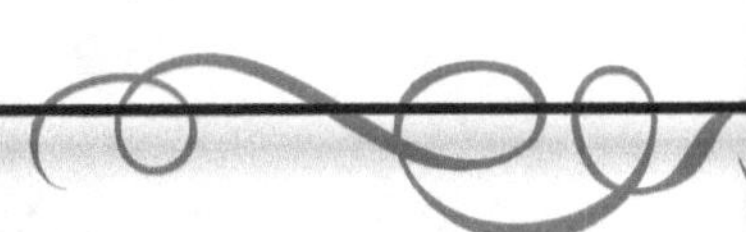

By: Janel Francis

Broken Brain, Healed Heart

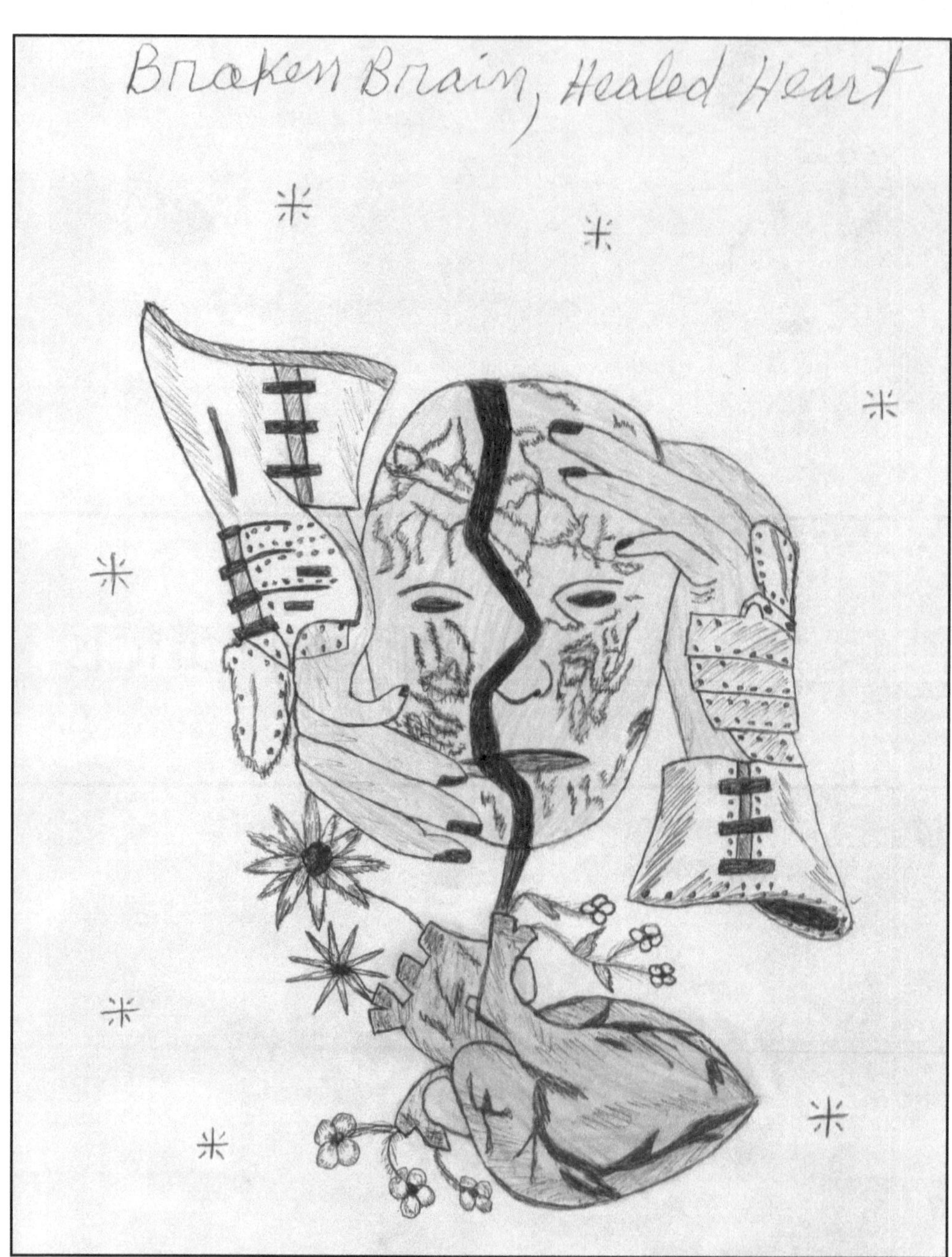

By: Robin Lunceford

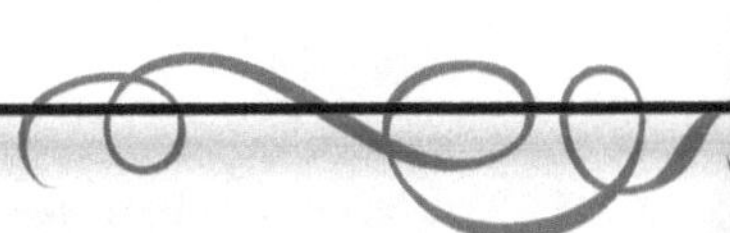

By: Warren Straniti

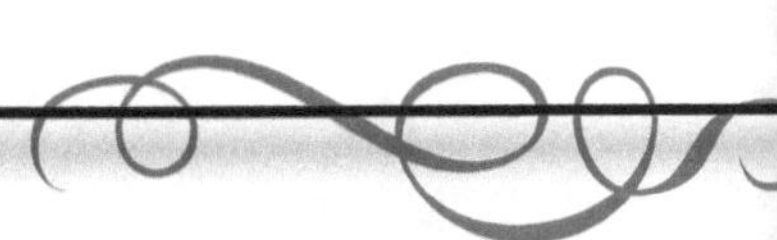

NOTE OF APPRECIATION:

Thanks to: Lucinda Jones, Savanna Jones, Winford Foley, Dorothy Foley, Jeffery Foley, Rita Smith, Mat Smith, Myron Smith, Heather Shively, Rick Castellani, Anthony Hodges, Kevin Cloud, Brandon Ledford, Matthew Warren, Bernard Reynolds, Alex Berger, Amy Smith, Tina Waltman, David Garcia, Thomas Crane, Demetrious Leonard Edwards Jr., Michael D. Watkins, Janel Francis, Robin Lunceford, Warren Straniti, Vicky Cuthbertson, Cassidy Parnell, etc. Thanks to: whoever I have forgotten to mention. Thanks to: God the Father, the Son Jesus Christ, and the Holy Spirit! Thanks to everybody who has inspired and encouraged me to be an author....

FORMERLY THE DISTORTED SOUL,
RICHARD LAYTON FOLEY

Email me at

<u>authorrichardfoley@gmail.com</u>

www.ingramcontent.com/pod-product-compliance
Lightning Source LLC
Chambersburg PA
CBHW031429250726
48656CB00002B/893